I Have Five Senses

Katie Sharp

Photographs by Ken O'Donoghue

A Harcourt Achieve Imprint

www.Rigby.com
1-800-531-5015

I walk.

I walk with Grandpa.

We walk and
hold hands.
I touch Grandpa's hand.
I touch with my hands.

It is time for sleeping.
I go to sleep at 8:00.
Good night!

We walk
down the street.
I hear cars.
I hear with my ears.

We walk to the park.

I see trees.

I see with my eyes.

We walk to the store.

I smell bread.

I smell with my nose.

We walk to the
ice cream store.
I taste ice cream.
I taste with my tongue.

13

We walk home.
I walk with Grandpa.

I am happy.
I have five senses!

16